Why Not, Lafayette?

JEAN FRITZ

Why Not, Lafayette?

illustrated by RONALD HIMLER

SCHOLASTIC INC.

New York Toronto London Auckland Sydney
Mexico City New Delhi Hong Kong

ISBN 0-439-27431-1

Text copyright © 1999 by Jean Fritz.
Illustrations copyright © 1999 by Ronald Himler. All rights reserved.
Published by Scholastic Inc., 555 Broadway, New York, NY 10012,
by arrangement G. P. Putnam's Sons, a division of Penguin Putnam Inc.
SCHOLASTIC and associated logos are trademarks and/or
registered trademarks of Scholastic Inc.

12 11 10 9 8 7 6 5 4 3 2 1   1 2 3 4 5 6/0

Printed in the U.S.A.   40

First Scholastic printing, March 2001

Designed by Marikka Tamura.
Text set in Garamond 3.

For Sandra Garrison, an instant friend,
who took me to the 240th birthday party
for Lafayette at Fayetteville, North Carolina.

My thanks go to Dr. Lloyd C. Kramer of
the University of North Carolina for his careful
and critical reading of my manuscript.

And thanks to Dr. Elizabeth Hostetler
for typing much of the manuscript.

Why Not, Lafayette?

✤ Chapter One ✤

His full name was Marie Joseph Paul Yves Roch Gilbert du Motier, Marquis de Lafayette. But no one called him that except maybe the priest on his baptism day. His family called him Gilbert. The boys at school called him Blondinet because he had spiky red hair and pale, freckled skin. When the men in the village saw him, they tipped their hats and called him Marquis. And what did Lafayette call himself? Just Lafayette. That was enough. His father had been killed in a battle in 1759, so there was only one Lafayette.

Soon after his father died, Lafayette's mother moved to Paris leaving her two-year-old son at their country home with his grandmother and his aunts and their never-ending supply of stories. "Glory" stories they were—about brave men and one woman who had won glory. The Lafayettes had relatives who had fought under Joan of Arc and she had a grand story.

Growing up Lafayette sometimes wondered if he'd ever have a story of his own. Then he heard about a monster that was loose in their neighborhood, killing animals and threatening babies. Here was his chance, he thought. He'd go in the woods and kill that monster with his bare hands. But too bad for glory. Someone else got there first and found there was no monster, after all. Only a wolf.

Sometimes Lafayette wondered if glory would show in a man's face after he'd won it. He looked hard at faces, but he never saw a drop of anything that looked like glory. Of course out in the country where he lived there weren't many faces to look at, but when he was eleven, his mother sent for him to come to Paris where there were thousands of faces. A person had to be careful because there were also thousands of feet and hundreds of whirring carriage wheels and prancing horses and Great Danes. (The Great Danes galloped ahead of the carriages—one to every carriage—like an advance guard of the army.) Not one person in Paris tipped his hat to an eleven-year-old boy even if he was a marquis.

It wasn't glory that his mother had in mind for Lafayette. It was a wife. Marriages were arranged by parents in those days and it wasn't too early to begin looking. Unfortunately, however, she died before she had picked out a wife. His grandfather died at about the same time, and suddenly there was Lafayette with a great deal of inherited money and a great many eligible young girls whose fathers were looking him over. Lafayette's great-grandfather, in charge of him now, had no trouble at all arranging a good marriage.

On April 11, 1774, Lafayette, now sixteen, married fourteen-year-old Adrienne of the noble Noailles family. She fell head over heels in love with Lafayette, and though he felt friendly toward her and called her "my dear heart," he was miserable. It was not his wife who was at fault, but his life. He was expected to go to balls at the palace (he didn't dance

well), to play tennis (he generally lost), and to gamble (which he despised). He wore his red hair in a short pigtail stuffed inside a little pigtail bag just as the other young men did and like them, he was expected to spend much of his time at court. He didn't even approve of the king and queen who threw money around without a thought for the many people in Paris who were hungry. Glory? The king was so short sighted, he would trip over glory without even knowing it was there.

Lafayette was bored. He wasn't <u>doing</u> anything, he complained. He was nineteen before he knew what he wanted to do. The year was 1776 and England and its American colonies were at war with each other. The more Lafayette heard about that war, the more he knew he belonged in America, fighting for freedom beside the Americans. He had always felt strongly about freedom. Once in school he was asked to describe the perfect horse. If the horse saw its master reach for his whip, the horse would throw its master, he wrote. Wasn't that just what America was doing? Throwing off its master?

In France a boy had to be twenty-five before he came of age, so of course in order to fight in a foreign war, Lafayette would need permission from his father-in-law and from the king. He knew what they would say: NO. So he decided to make his arrangements in secret. He didn't even tell Adrienne, who was expecting their second child. (They already had Henriette.) But he did tell the two representatives from America, Silas Deane and Benjamin Franklin.

How did he expect to get to America? Mr. Deane asked.

He'd provide a ship out of his own money, Lafayette replied.

In that case, Mr. Deane said, he would make him a major general in the American army. (Mr. Deane loved to turn Frenchmen into American officers.)

Benjamin Franklin wrote to George Washington, asking him to look out for the "boy." (Because he looked even younger than his years, Lafayette was often referred to as the "boy.")

However, before Lafayette's ship, the *Victoire,* was ready news of his plans leaked out in Paris. His father-in-law was furious and ordered Lafayette to join his family immediately for a long vacation in Italy.

Italy! Lafayette scoffed at the suggestion. Imagine him "dragging out a life without glory in the midst of persons opposed" to his way of thinking! It was about this time that he remembered an ancestor who had fought with Joan of Arc. His motto had been: *"Cur non?"* or "Why not?" Lafayette decided to adopt the same motto, and he put it on his family crest. "Why not?" It was his personal reply to all the No's that had been thrown in his path.

The *Victoire* set sail on April 20, 1777, with ten young Frenchmen who, like Lafayette, wanted to fight for America. Once out at sea, they must have felt they were safe from the king, but the ocean rose up, as if it were acting on royal orders, attacking the little ship so mercilessly the men had to be tied in their hammocks to keep from being flung into Kingdom Come (wherever that was). For fifty-four days they rolled and heaved and swung in their hammocks until they finally sighted land. Flat and solid, in one place.

It turned out to be the coast of South Carolina, but more important, it was AMERICA and Lafayette fell in love with it. Everything was better here, he boasted: the people were more friendly, the cities more handsome, the women prettier. When he and his friends set out for Philadelphia, they discovered, however, the road was nothing to brag about. Often it was simply not there. "According to his usual praiseworthy custom," he said, his carriage broke down, his horse went lame. But worst of all were the mosquitoes—battalions of mosquitoes that lay in ambush as if they were in the pay of the enemy.

Lafayette swatted and scratched, scratched and swatted. Well, he admitted, every country had some faults, and he supposed in America it was mosquitoes. In any case, for thirty-two days the men trudged on until at last they reached Philadelphia and knocked on the door of the Continental Congress.

Here they were! they announced. New officers for the American army.

The representative who opened the door understood French perfectly. The American army needed no new French officers, he snapped, no matter what Silas Deane had told them.

Lafayette wrote to the president of the Congress, John Hancock. Could he not serve as a volunteer? he asked. Without pay?

He was accepted.

The next day he met George Washington. There was no mistaking him. He stood tall, a commanding presence, with glory written all over him. This was the man Lafayette had been looking for all his life. Like everyone else, Washington seemed to like Lafayette. But what was he to do with a nineteen-year-old major general who knew nothing of America?

He decided to invite him to stay at his headquarters where Lafayette quickly made friends with other members of Washington's staff—Colonel Alexander Hamilton, for instance, and the corpulent Henry Knox, who loved not only to eat, but to talk about food. Lafayette and Knox spent hours in camp, imagining the grand dishes they would serve if they could.

On August 20, Lafayette sat with top-ranking officers at his first council of war. Two hundred ships of the British fleet had just landed in Chesapeake Bay, close enough to make the citizens of Philadelphia nervous. To raise their spirits, Washington ordered the army to parade through Philadelphia. "The army is to march in one column," he said. "The drums and fifes of each brigade are to be collected in the center of it and a tune for the quick-step played, but with such moderation that the men may step to it with ease, and without <u>dancing along</u> as has been too often the case."

Once the parade had formed, Lafayette looked back at the long column of men. Of course without regular uniforms they looked a bit shabby in their hunting shirts, but this was the American Army, Lafayette told himself. See how smartly they stepped out!

Heading the parade was General Washington on horseback with General Lafayette riding beside him, probably on a white horse for he was partial to white horses. The people of Philadelphia had turned out to see the parade, but they seemed most interested in the young French officer right up front with their commander.

✤ Chapter Two ✤

Of course it was wonderful leading a parade beside General Washington, but, still, it wasn't glory. And there was no chance of glory while he was a major general in name only. He needed men to command and action to direct. He longed to throw himself against the eighteen hundred British troops who had just landed in Chesapeake Bay, heading for Philadelphia, but all he could do was follow along. Washington was determined to keep the British from crossing Brandywine Creek. He had units stationed at every ford, but which ford would they try to cross? Washington received so many contradictory reports, he didn't dare move until he was sure. He waited too long.

Suddenly the news came. The British had already crossed the creek at the point that General Sullivan was trying to defend. Lafayette turned to Washington.

Could he go and help General Sullivan?

Washington nodded. So away Lafayette galloped. No one knew then, not even Lafayette himself, that he was a born leader, that somehow he had the ability to inspire men to do what he wanted. General Sullivan's forces were already retreating as Lafayette rushed into their midst. Unmindful of danger, he set such an example of bravery that the Americans followed him, at least until the enemy came within twenty yards. Only then did they flee in panic.

But not Lafayette. He had been hit, but either he did not know it, or he chose not to pay any attention until someone pointed to his boot and the blood pouring out of it. By this time Washington had joined Lafayette, and when he saw Lafayette had been hit, he ordered him to get down from his horse and have his wound attended to.

"Treat him as though he were my son," Washington told the doctors.

Lafayette wrote Adrienne: "The better I know him [Washington], the more I venerate him—[he] has been kind enough to become my intimate friend. We live together like two devoted brothers in mutual intimacy. The friendship makes me most happy in this country. When he sent his chief surgeon to me, he told him to care for me as though I were his son, because he loves me as much as a son."

Washington instructed him to stay in his hospital quarters until his wound was completely healed. Lafayette tried to obey but his wound healed slowly, and all the time the war was going on without him. After three months he could stay still no longer. Although he still couldn't get his boot on, he went limping back to duty.

He was there, ready for action when the British, now in command of Philadelphia, marched into New Jersey to raid American farms. Like everyone else, Lafayette couldn't bear the idea of the British stuffing themselves on stolen American food. It was hard enough to think of the British living it up in high style in Philadelphia—attending parties, balls, dressing according to the latest fashion, the ladies piling their hair so high that they often had to hang their heads out of their carriage windows. General Howe, the British commander in chief, seemed to be having the best time of all.

The American army, on the other hand, at their winter quarters in Valley Forge just outside Philadelphia, was destitute without clothes, shoes, food, and shivering from the cold in ramshackle huts. Of course the Americans wanted to stop the British raids on American farms. And if they couldn't stop them, they would at least give the British a hard time. That's what Lafayette meant to do.

Lafayette was high spirited and often impulsive, but as a warrior he was cool and calculating, acting just as he thought Washington would want him to. So when he and his three hundred men came across a nest of well-fed, unsuspecting Hessian soldiers fighting for the British, he saw he was not only outnumbered, but poorly positioned. Quietly his men circled the Hessians before taking action, but when they struck, they struck hard, killing and scattering the entire band. As a result, some Philadelphians did not have as much beef or as many chickens as they had expected. On the other hand, the Hessians, with their crude table manners, were not there to share the feast. (One Hessian general was said to spread the butter on his bread with his thumb.)

And where was General Lafayette now? Back at camp, he was cheered by the American troops. And he was officially made a major general in the army with a unit of his own, such as it was. Like other units, it was poorly equipped, so Lafayette,

using his own money, ordered uniforms and boots for every man under him.

All was not well with Washington, however, nor, as it turned out, with Lafayette. A small group of men headed by General Gates, who had been in command at America's one big victory at Saratoga, had decided Washington was too slow; he should be replaced as commander in chief by General Gates. Moreover, the team of Washington and Lafayette should be broken up. This conspiracy of men set up what they called the Board of War, which was to be in charge of military matters. At first they tried to persuade Lafayette to go back to Paris. He had won his glory, they argued. Why not go back and enjoy his fame and family?

Well, why not? Lafayette asked himself. He was often homesick. Still, there was something suspicious about this suggestion, but when these same men offered him a chance to lead an expedition to Canada, it was another story. Why not? he asked himself again. Here was his Big Chance. He'd always wanted to make a direct hit at England. He'd even dreamed of invading England itself. But one thing must be clear, he insisted: his would not be an independent command. He'd report directly to Washington.

That was no problem, he was told. He was promised everything. Three thousand armed men would be waiting for him in Albany. Congress would provide four hundred thousand dollars. It seems strange that no one in Pennsylvania warned him winter might not be the best time to conquer Canada. But as soon as he and his small group of aides took off on horseback, Lafayette could see the weather was against them. That was just the beginning. When he finally reached his destination (February 17, 1778), he wrote Washington in his not-yet-perfect English: "I met Albany," he said. It didn't sound like a happy meeting.

And it wasn't. Instead of the three thousand men he'd been promised, he found only a few militia without adequate clothes, food, or armament. And no money from Congress. The generals who were already in the North shook their heads. What a crazy idea, they said, to set off for Canada in this weather! Lafayette felt like a fool. If the American generals laughed at him, what would his French friends say?

"Oh, General Washington," he cried, "why am I so far away from you?"

At the height of his discouragement, Washington recalled him, so he was back in Valley Forge when the Big News arrived. In April 1778, a ship from France brought an official announcement that a treaty of alliance had been signed between the United States and France. America was no longer in the war alone. Lafayette was so excited he flung his arms around General Washington and, in the French fashion, kissed him soundly on both cheeks. Washington hated any display of intimacy. Indeed, he had once scolded Alexander Hamilton for slapping him playfully on the shoulder. But for Lafayette, he stood his ground until the embrace was over. Then the two friends shook hands and congratulated each other on their good fortune.

Everyone wondered what the English would do now that France was in the war. The first thing they did was get rid of General Howe. They gave his place as commander in chief to Sir Henry Clinton. And what, the Americans asked, were they to expect from Clinton?

Washington told Lafayette to find out. With two thousand troops Lafayette went to the village of Barren Hill, a good spot for reconnoitering. What he didn't know was that a spy had informed the British of Lafayette's plan. The British laughed. Now they would catch the "boy!" So sure were they that they sent dinner invitations to the leaders of Philadelphia society, promising to bring Lafayette to the dinner and introduce him to all the guests. After all, they just had to surround the "boy," creep up on him from all sides, and pull him in as if they were catching a fish in their net. Accordingly, they set about their business.

George Washington, looking through his field glasses from a rise of ground at Valley Forge, saw what was happening and ordered warning shots to be fired. But Lafayette didn't need the warning. He saw what the British were doing, and fortunately he knew of a secret path that led from Barren Hill down to the river. He sent his troops ahead, then bringing up the rear, he followed them back to Valley Forge.

And when the British generals arrived at Barren Hill, all they saw were other British generals. No fish. No "boy." And no guest of honor for the ladies waiting in Philadelphia.

But the British weren't going to waste any more time on a cocky young French general. A French fleet was on its way to America, and the British knew they shouldn't hang around Philadelphia any longer. General Clinton sent a major part of his army, nine thousand strong along with a baggage train of fifteen hundred wagons, through New Jersey toward New York.

Washington and his army followed. Among the officers was one whom Lafayette did not know, General Charles Lee. He had a fine reputation as a warrior, but was an unpleasant man. He loved his dogs who accompanied him wherever he went, but he didn't care much for people. Lafayette, who made friends easily, took an immediate dislike to Lee, but since Lee outranked him, he knew he'd be serving under him.

✤ Chapter Three ✤

On July 24, 1778 near the town of Monmouth, New Jersey, Washington decided to force a confrontation with the British. It was such an unbearably hot day that men were dropping to the ground almost as if they were already in battle. They should act quickly, Washington said; they should attack the enemy's rear. The American officers agreed with Washington, all but General Lee. Play it safe, he said. Nevertheless, he was overruled, and he took command, or so everyone thought. But at the last minute he changed his mind. He didn't want to do this. Of course Lafayette was pleased. He was next in line to command, and he figured this might turn out to be a glory time.

Then Lee changed his mind again. And again. What was he up to? Lafayette asked himself. Advancing one minute, backing up the next, getting his men into total confusion. Lee's dogs could have done a better job. And now Lee was actually retreating. Lafayette sent a messenger to tell Washington to come to the front.

Everything stopped as Washington galloped into sight, looking like a thunderstorm about to break.

"What is the meaning of this?" he cried to Lee.

"American troops," Lee replied, "would not stand up to British bayonets."

The thunder broke. "You damn poltroon!" Washington shouted. "You haven't tried them." Lafayette had never heard Washington swear before, but obviously he could. He sent Lee to the rear as if he were a child being sent to his room.

Then Lafayette and Washington reorganized Lee's men and while Washington rode up and down beside the line, the fighting resumed. It was a back-and-forth affair. One side would gain a little ground, then the other. At the end of the day no one had won, but both armies were too overcome with weariness to continue. They withdrew from one another and lay down on the ground. Washington spread out his cloak, and he and Lafayette shared it, looking up at the night sky, brushing away mosquitoes, and talking about General Lee.

In the middle of the night the British army quietly slipped away, so that was the end of the Battle of Monmouth. But it was not the end of Charles Lee. He wrote obnoxious letters, insisting on his innocence, bragging that a court martial would clear his name. He got the court martial he wanted, but was declared guilty and discharged from the army. In the backwoods of Virginia he found a windowless shack and moved in with his dogs. When he died in 1782, two of his dogs were lying on either side of him, refusing to move.

With the French in the war, Lafayette wondered if he shouldn't be fighting for France. After all, if France made some dramatic move against England, he would want to be a part of it. Meanwhile he was excited to think of his own countrymen fighting beside him.

When he wrote to welcome Count d'Estaing, admiral of the French fleet, his language took on a boyish enthusiasm he didn't show to Americans. "I love to think that you will deliver the first blows to an impudent nation [England]," he wrote. "May you do them as much harm as they wish us."

Washington and Lafayette, as well as most of the army, took for granted the final deciding battle would take place in New York, which was held by the British. But not yet. The French ships were so heavily loaded they couldn't get into New York Harbor. So Washington sent them to Newport, Rhode Island, which the British were also holding. And he sent Lafayette along to help the commander, General Sullivan, against the British.

Again Lafayette wrote to d'Estaing. In a froth of joy over joining the French, his words bubbled over each other. "Nothing," he said, "that has ever been announced to me since I have been on earth has given me more pleasure."

But suppose he did not arrive before the action began? "In the name of your own love of glory," he wrote, "do not begin before we arrive. . . . I avow that if I were to arrive too late, I should wish to hang myself."

Lafayette was not the only one who dreamed of glory; most of the leaders at Newport seemed to be dreaming. General Sullivan said he wasn't ready to join the French; his militia hadn't come. D'Estaing couldn't wait to start. A quick attack would be the most successful. Day after day Sullivan still wasn't ready. Then General Greene arrived on the scene. Greene's home was in Rhode Island, and he wanted glory in his own state. So there was jealousy all around. Lafayette was kept busy running from one party to another, mediating, which he did very well and would do all his life. While he tried to calm all the short tempers, Lafayette himself was anything but calm. Ever since the French had arrived, he had been in a fever of excitement. "Half the Americans," he confided in a letter to Adrienne, "say that I have gone mad. . . . Between you and me, they are somewhat right; I have never felt so strongly the sense of national pride."

But an agreement was finally reached. Americans and French were to attack the British together so the glory would be shared. The attack was to take place on August 8, a day that was blanketed with fog. But d'Estaing was in for a surprise. Sullivan had started ahead of him. The British, Sullivan explained, had abandoned key positions, and he had simply taken possession.

Then came another surprise. The fog suddenly lifted and out at sea loomed a whole line of British ships bearing down on Newport. D'Estaing knew what he had to do now. He turned his ships around and went after the British, but the ships had scarcely disappeared from sight when a storm blew up. It was a gigantic storm that raged at the ships, inflicting more damage to the two fleets than they could have done to each other. It was ten days before d'Estaing came limping back to Newport in his crippled flagship.

But d'Estaing was not staying. He had sealed orders from the king that if the fleet needed repair, he was to go directly to Boston. Lafayette, in order to make sure the repairs were made quickly, rode the seventy miles to Boston in seven hours. But Sullivan was furious, declaring that from now on, Americans should learn to take care of themselves; they couldn't depend on allies.

Lafayette, still riding high on his national pride, took offense. No matter what France did, he declared, France was always right, and he threatened to challenge Sullivan to a duel. Washington talked him out of it. Duels were out of fashion, he said, and Lafayette would only be laughed at.

But if the expedition at Newport fizzled out, Lafayette had not fizzled. His friendship with d'Estaing had fed all his most ambitious dreams. Attack Canada? D'Estaing was all for it. They talked of putting Canadian cities, one after another, in flames. And England itself. If d'Estaing were ever asked to invade England, Lafayette begged to go with him. If the French went there without him, he said, he would "hang himself."

First, of course, he'd have to go back to France to see what its plans were and to determine if he should fight with the French army. Washington agreed he should take a leave of absence from the army, and while he was in France he could petition for more supplies and money. But not more men. The American army might not accept too many more Frenchmen.

Lafayette may not have realized how much of an American he had become until he boarded the ship that was to take him home. All at once he was overcome with homesickness. Even while the sails were being raised, he wrote one last note to Washington.

"I hope I shall see you soon again," he wrote, "and tell you myself with what emotion I now leave the coast you inhabit."

✦ Chapter Four ✦

Lafayette did not know what to expect when he reached France in February of 1779. After all, he had left against the orders of the king and was due to be punished. What kind of punishment? he wondered. As it turned out, however, he was only confined to his own home for ten days, allowed to see no one outside his family and denied contact with the king. Actually, he was pleased for the chance to be alone with his family. His little daughter, Henriette, had died during his absence, but now there was a second daughter, Anastasie, born soon after Lafayette reached America.

But when his so-called isolation ended, it *really* ended. He couldn't go out on the street without being mobbed, followed, and cheered. "The Hero of the New World" he was called. He thought perhaps his uniform was causing undue attention, so he took to wearing civilian clothes. It made no difference. He couldn't even go to a public performance—a play or a concert—without being given a standing ovation. When it was suggested he avoid public appearances since they interfered with performances, he did what he liked best. He spent his time talking with officials about the American war, suggesting daring schemes for defeating England. What about raids on the English coast? What about stirring up trouble in Ireland so the English would be distracted? What about invading Canada? He got nowhere with these ideas, but he did manage to get material help. He wanted so much the king laughed. Lafayette would like to take everything out of the palace, he said, and give it to the Americans.

"I would," Lafayette admitted.

Indeed, he seemed to think less of glory these days than he did of liberty. He wanted America to win the war not only because he liked winning, but because he had become wholly devoted to the American idea that people should have a say in their government. If America established such a government, he thought, countries in Europe might follow their example. Why not? Perhaps this would be the beginning of a more perfect world.

Lafayette was in France for a year, from February 1779 to March 1780, and though he was given many opportunities to celebrate, there were two occasions he particularly treasured. First, on behalf of the American Congress, Benjamin Franklin presented him with a special sword with a gold hilt. It was engraved with his coat of arms and his motto—*Why not?*— and with representations of each of the military actions in which he had taken part. On one side of the handle was a medallion showing Lafayette, sword in hand, stepping on the neck of a lion, representing Great Britain. On the other side was a figure of Liberty holding up a broken chain while handing Lafayette a branch of laurel.

But the most wonderful surprise came on Christmas Eve. Adrienne gave birth to a son. Lafayette knew immediately what to name the boy. Indeed, there could be only one name—George Washington de Lafayette.

Meanwhile, the war was not going well in America. The English had captured Savannah, Georgia, as well as Charleston, South Carolina, where they had taken more than five thousand prisoners and their commanding officer, General Benjamin Lincoln. In letters Washington never said directly how bad the situation was, but reading between the lines, Lafayette could see he needed all the help he could get—even French soldiers. So the French were sending six thousand men, but they were keeping it a secret.

Naturally, Lafayette wanted to be in command of the six thousand, and he tried one argument after another to get his way. Any other French commander, he said, would not know how to humor Congress; Americans could be difficult. In addition, each state had its own peculiarity. A commander could not, for instance, talk to an officer from Boston in the same way he might talk to someone from Newport or Poughkeepsie. Lafayette really did understand Americans better than other foreigners, not just the peculiarities of where they came from. He appreciated how they fought and why they fought. He entered into their thinking as if he weren't even a stranger.

The French, however, were afraid of stirring up trouble in their own army if they gave the command to Lafayette. No matter how popular he was, he was still only twenty-two years old. So the king appointed a veteran to the command—the Count de Rochambeau (often called "Papa Rochambeau" behind his back). Lafayette, however, was to go to America first so he could prepare Washington for the arrival of the French army.

No one in America knew Lafayette was coming until he suddenly docked at Boston. People went wild with excitement. John Hancock, who often served as governor of Massachusetts when he wasn't president of the Continental Congress, gave one of the huge parties for which he was famous. The party spilled out of his house and onto Boston Common where bonfires and firecrackers lit up the night.

Just as Lafayette had expected, Washington was relieved to know a French army would be arriving. He sent Lafayette to notify Congress of their coming and then to Newport where Rochambeau was expected. "All the information he [Lafayette] gives," Washington wrote Rochambeau, "all the propositions he makes, I entreat you to consider as coming from me." What Washington wanted was an immediate attack on New York where the British were holed in, where, as Lafayette knew, the final battle had to be fought.

Rochambeau obviously did not like the idea of an immediate attack on New York. Moreover, he did not like discussing military strategy with a man young enough to be his grandson. He must have a personal interview with Washington who was encamped now in New Jersey and did not want to go to Rhode Island to see Rochambeau. In any case, Lafayette would have to act as an interpreter between the two men. In the end a compromise was reached. Lafayette, mediating again, arranged for the two parties to meet on September 20 at Hartford, Connecticut.

Generals Knox, Hamilton, and Lafayette were in Washington's party while Rochambeau was accompanied by his staff. They came together in the public square before the courthouse at Hartford but then proceeded to a private house

where they talked for two days. It was clear to all present that the situation was desperate. Lord Cornwallis had just defeated General Gates in a bloody battle at Camden, South Carolina; Americans were deserting right and left; the British controlled the seas; Clinton was at New York; Cornwallis held Georgia, the Carolinas, and Virginia. So it was not hard for Washington and Rochambeau to reach an agreement: France would simply have to send more ships, men, and money. The message was sent swiftly.

On the way back to his headquarters, Washington suggested they take a look at the fort at West Point which was under the command of General Benedict Arnold. The Arnolds lived in a private house across the river from the fort and were at breakfast when Hamilton and the young American doctor, McHenry, arrived to inform the Arnolds that Washington would be along shortly. During breakfast, however, a message was delivered to Arnold. Obviously upset, Arnold pushed back his chair and said he had to go to the fort but would be back in an hour. He must have had time for a private word with Mrs. Arnold, for she left the table hastily and went upstairs.

This was the puzzling situation when Washington and Lafayette arrived. They ate a bit of breakfast, then crossed the river to find Arnold. He wasn't there. So they returned only to hear that a spy had been caught and was being held at West Point. Hamilton left to find out the details.

"It's Major Andre!" he reported on his return. This was no small-time spy. Major Andre was the adjutant general under Clinton. And he had been found with a map of West Point in his boot and papers in the handwriting of Arnold. Hamilton set out to overtake Arnold but didn't make it. Arnold had already managed to escape on board the British man-of-war, the *Vulture,* at anchor in the Hudson.

It was impossible to hang Arnold (as they longed to do), but they did have to hang Andre (which they didn't want to do). Andre was well liked, a personable, brave young man. Lafayette was one of the officers assigned to try his case, but when the time came for the hanging, neither Lafayette nor Washington joined the crowd of spectators who had come to see the sight. Instead they both stayed in their rooms and pulled down their shades.

The next they heard of Arnold, he was a brevet-brigadier general in the British army, and was in command of two thousand men attacking Virginia. Washington sent Lafayette to capture him and bring him back, preferably alive so they could string him up as they had once wanted to do. Unfortunately, Arnold got away.

Now Lafayette wanted to get back North quickly so he could be on hand to help Washington and Rochambeau attack New York. Instead, Washington sent him to Virginia to stop an advance by Cornwallis, the best general in the British army who had at his command five times the number of men that Lafayette had.

Holding out no hope for his success, Lafayette wrote he was "devilishly busy getting himself licked." To Washington he wrote: "I am not strong enough even to be beaten." Cornwallis gloated: "The boy cannot escape me."

"The boy" wanted only to be with Washington, preparing to attack New York. His men, mostly from New England and hating the South, also wanted to go North. When Lafayette learned they were secretly planning to desert, he called them together. He was facing a most difficult problem, he explained, and if anyone wanted to go North, he would be glad to give him written permission so he would not get in trouble. Lafayette had already earned the name of "the soldier's friend" and this latest appeal endeared him further. There was no more talk of desertion.

In order to avoid a battle he would necessarily lose, Lafayette led his men on a zigzag, round-about path as if he were creating a child's puzzle across the map of Virginia. On June 10, however, General Mad Anthony Wayne with nine hundred Pennsylvanians found his way into the puzzle and joined Lafayette. With this many reinforcements, Lafayette quit his puzzle game and turned on Cornwallis. To his surprise, Cornwallis also changed direction as if it were his turn to be on the run. Lafayette's army continued to grow the farther he went until he had an army of five thousand.

Both armies moved quickly, the Americans on the heels of the British. Cornwallis was in and out of Richmond one day; Lafayette was in and out the next day. It was an eleven hundred-mile chase with Lafayette blocking Cornwallis' escape to the west and Cornwallis racing toward the sea, ending up right on the coast at Yorktown.

While Cornwallis expected Clinton to send ships down from New York to rescue him, Lafayette didn't know what to expect. He wrote Washington, describing the lay of the land, the rivers and swamps surrounding Yorktown. "If a fleet of ours would enter the bay," he said, "our affairs would turn for the best."

Then one day a letter came from Washington telling him

under no circumstances to come North. There would be no command to give him. A French fleet under Count de Grasse was leaving the West Indies for the Chesapeake region to join forces against Cornwallis. There would be, Washington said, "aid from this quarter." Did that mean Washington was coming South? Lafayette marveled. The final battle would not be in New York, after all. It would be *here*!

"I heartily thank you," Lafayette wrote to Washington, "for having ordered me to remain in Virginia."

Washington was sending his army out in small battalions so Clinton would think they were on their way to a common meeting ground for a New York attack. The men, themselves, did not know their destination and made bets with each other about where they were going. Meanwhile, Washington and Rochambeau were heading south, but the French fleet got there first, ready to fight immediately. It sounded to Lafayette like a repeat of the Newport debacle, and he had to use all his mediating powers to get the French to wait for Washington. They couldn't wait, the French insisted. This was hurricane season in the West Indies; they had to get back in a hurry. There was no compromise in Lafayette. No, he said again and again. This was General Washington's war, and if this battle turned out to be the finish of it, he had to be there.

So they waited. Perhaps it was now that Lafayette was making secret plans with Jim, the slave who had been lent to him to serve as a valet and groom. Posing as a black runaway, Jim was to cross into enemy territory, pick up what news he could and report back to Lafayette. He did such a good job that after the war, Lafayette persuaded Virginia to free him. Jim, who, like most slaves, had no last name in English, adopted the name *Lafayette* which he used for life.

Another man who worked for Lafayette became his friend—his bodyguard, Isham Blake, from North Carolina. Isham was a fifer and always had music running around his head. If he wasn't playing his fife, he was whistling. Half under his breath he whistled, which made Lafayette laugh. If he didn't hear that whistle, he'd worry about what had happened to his bodyguard.

Then at four o'clock in the afternoon on September 28, Washington and Rochambeau rode down the road where Lafayette was waiting. For once, it seemed everything was going according to plan. All the parties who were expected were there, and their combined forces outnumbered those of Cornwallis.

On September 28, the whole army moved forward to Yorktown where Cornwallis was barricaded, still hoping for help from Clinton. The Americans and French organized themselves for a siege with Lafayette in command of the right wing and Alexander Hamilton serving under him. While cannons roared night and day, the Americans and French proceeded from one line of redoubts to another until there were only two crucial redoubts left. It was late at night, and it was raining. If they continued, could they keep their powder dry? They continued. Hamilton climbed on the shoulders of his men and threw himself over the top of the redoubt. His men followed, and the war turned into a hand-to-hand affair with a terrible slashing of bayonets. It was over in ten minutes and that, in effect, was the end of the Battle of Yorktown.

On October 17, a drummer came out of the English headquarters, signaling with his drums that they wanted to negotiate. Washington would have nothing to do with negotiations. He demanded a complete surrender, and after a few hours the British agreed.

On Friday morning, October 19, 1781, the American flag flew over that last redoubt. The Americans and French formed two lines which the defeated English had to pass through. Washington, Rochambeau, and their staffs, including Lafayette, rode to the middle of the line to receive the defeated army. Onlookers crowded at the edge of the scene in silence. Washington had given orders that there would be no cheering.

Cornwallis, however, was not in the lead as had been expected. He was said to be sick so he sent his second in command who presented his sword to Rochambeau, as if he were the commander in chief. This was his way of snubbing the Americans and giving the French credit for winning the war. Rochambeau refused the sword. Shaking his head, he nodded in the direction of Washington, who in turn sent him to General Lincoln who had suffered the humiliation of being captured by the British at Charlestown. Lincoln accepted the sword, but immediately returned it.

Two more years would pass before a peace treaty was signed, but everyone recognized that America had won its war. For Lafayette this was not only a victory over England, it was a personal victory—a life decision. From now on he would dedicate himself to pursue liberty wherever it might lead him. But at the moment it was time for him to go to Philadelphia and apply for another leave of absence.

Washington wrote to him before he sailed: "I owe it to your friendship and to my affectionate regard for you, my dear Marquis, not to let you leave this country without carrying with you fresh marks of my attachment to you."

Lafayette responded: *"Adieu,* my dear General, I know your heart so well that I am sure no distance can alter your attachment to me. My love, my respect, my gratitude for you are above expression."

✤ Chapter Five ✤

Once Lafayette was in France, he and Washington corresponded regularly, sprinkling their letters with requests of each other. Washington wondered if Lafayette could send him a donkey, and perhaps because Lafayette liked to think of a little French donkey grazing at Mt. Vernon, he sent not only a donkey but also two mares. Gifts went back and forth—a red partridge and a foxhound from Lafayette; hams and ducks from Washington. There was one thing Lafayette wished he had. He had fallen in love with the mockingbird in America. Europe had no mockingbirds, and no matter how he tried to describe a mockingbird's song, he could never do it justice. Actually, the mockingbird had a large repertoire of songs, all of them triumphant. It was as if it were letting the world know its joy at being alive.

Lafayette and Adrienne bought a house in Paris and moved the family there—Anastasie, George, and now Virginie, born in 1783. He hung a framed copy of the Declaration of Independence on the wall, but left an empty space beside it. And what was the empty space for? his friends asked. It was reserved for a copy of the Rights of Man when such a document was adopted in France.

Every Monday night at the new house was "American night." Lafayette sent invitations written in English, expected conversation to be conducted in English and although some Frenchmen might be included in the guest list, they were invariably known to be sympathetic to America. And of course his American friends were invited—Franklin while he was there, and later Thomas Jefferson, a favorite.

Talk often centered on politics, on the growing financial troubles of France, but they also discussed the latest fads in Paris: hot air balloons, for instance, and the magic inventions of Dr. Mesmer from Vienna who claimed to be able to cure illnesses with the use of animal magnetism. Lafayette was impressed, at least until he read Dr. Mesmer's advice for seasickness. The seasick victim, Dr. Mesmer said, should wrap his arms tightly around the mainmast of the ship. Lafayette, who knew about seasickness, laughed. Had Dr. Mesmer never gone to sea? he asked. Didn't he know the lower portion of the mainmast is covered with tar?

The peace treaty between Great Britain and America was signed in September, 1783, and the following spring Lafayette went to America for a short visit. He spent two "perfect" weeks at Mt. Vernon with Washington—one of the few times the two friends had a chance to talk themselves out. He ate Mrs. Washington's fried chicken, which he liked so much he took the recipe home to Adrienne.

Lafayette was almost twenty-seven now, and he had the assurance of a man who knew what he wanted to do with his life. His American years had made all the difference. It was as if he had not only been plunged into the very stuff of liberty, but had been swished around in it until he was soaked through. Some people said he had been "influenced" by America; others said he had been "contaminated." Everyone knew he wanted the people of France to rule themselves the way the people of America did. The only difference would be that France would have a king, but the king would not be able to do anything he wanted. He'd have to obey a constitution.

Some reforms Lafayette decided he could try right away. Slavery, for instance. He had seen slavery at work in Virginia and he had hated it. France had no slaves, but there were slaves in French Guyana, and he could do something about that. He bought two plantations complete with slaves and set up a system whereby the slaves, after some initial training, would be freed.

Then there were the Protestants. France was a Catholic country with no tolerance for people of other faiths. Protestants could not legally marry; if they had children, they would be illegitimate. Lafayette visited a center where Protestants had settled and encouraged them to believe a day was coming when they'd all be equal. Indeed Lafayette adopted the motto that would become the watchword in France—Liberty, Equality, Fraternity. But instead of "fraternity," Lafayette substituted "order." When the people of France decided they wanted liberty, he didn't want them to go wild.

But they did go wild. When money became so scarce there wasn't enough to go around, women in Paris took to the streets, beating drums and crying, "Bread! Bread!" The people were angry, and if they made enough fuss they thought maybe the king would do something about it.

And what did the king do? He raised taxes on ordinary people so the wealthy people, including the queen and himself, would have more money. Riots broke out all over France and the king, thinking the aristocrats (or Second Estate) might help him out with money, called together an Assembly of Notables. Lafayette was, of course, one of the aristocrats, only he called it an assembly of "not ables." Still, he thought this might be a good time to try to change the government. At one of the first meetings of the assembly, he stood up and moved that all the people of France should participate in the government. Elections should be held for representatives among the clergy and especially among the common people (called the Third Estate). There was a dead silence in the room. Members glanced at each other, as if to say: "There he goes again! American ideas!"

Some people said this was the beginning of the French Revolution, and it was only two years before the king did call for elections all over the country for what would be known as the National Assembly. Unfortunately, at about the same time the king dismissed one of his most popular advisors, which set off another round of violence. On the night of July 14, 1789, a mob stormed the Bastille, the prison where political prisoners were kept. Lafayette jumped on his white horse, which the people had named Jean LeBlanc, and rode to the Bastille. In America he had learned how to talk to unhappy soldiers, how to make people believe in him. He was able to quiet the crowd, and in order to show what he thought of the

Bastille, he ordered it to be burned. The next day someone proposed that an independent National Guard should be formed to police Paris. And who should head the National Guard? The people were unanimous: and so was the National Assembly. They appointed Lafayette.

And why not? It would be like having his own army, but instead of making war, he would be keeping peace. For the next three years Lafayette rode at the head of his guard from one trouble spot to another and when the people saw him, they'd shout, *"Vive Lafayette!"* And sometimes they would add, *"Vive Jean LeBlanc!"*

In order to keep peace, Lafayette couldn't take sides; he had to protect everyone. This required a lot of mediating. Even so, he was suspected of favoring one side over another. Sometimes some of the common people thought he supported the king too strongly. Many aristocrats, as well as the king and queen, thought he leaned too far toward the common people. Indeed, in 1789, when he first presented his Declaration of the Rights of Man, written with the help of Thomas Jefferson, the queen accused him of being a "traitor to his class." In spite of all this controversy, Lafayette remained optimistic. Liberty was the right to speak and act according to one's conscience, and he believed it would eventually triumph over chaos. Even when chaos became more and more threatening, he didn't abandon hope.

Real danger, however, was brewing behind the scenes. A group of radical extremists wanted a republic with no king or queen, no aristocrats. They didn't care a thing about the traditional order of kings and aristocrats. The only way to deal with aristocrats, they believed, was to do away with them.

Later they would set up a contraption on the streets of Paris designed to execute enemies quickly and efficiently. Called a guillotine in honor of its inventor, Dr. Guillotin, it consisted of a board on which the victim was tied, a hole through which the victim inserted his head, and a sharp blade which was dropped on the victim's neck. The decapitated head fell into a waiting basket. Not wanting to part with their heads, aristocrats were fleeing France as fast as they could. Taking refuge in neighboring countries, they persuaded them, one by one, to make war on France. After all, who in Europe wanted to see such radical ideas spread?

On August 10, 1792, the extreme radicals seized complete power and ordered the arrest of Lafayette. He was thirty-four years old now and certainly he didn't want his head to end up in a basket, so he'd have to escape. His plan was to go to neutral Belgium, then on to Holland where he would take a ship to England. His family would meet him there, and they would all go to America. If he was stopped at any hostile outpost, he'd tell them not to worry. He'd soon be out of their way.

He was stopped by Austrian guards, and they didn't care about his excuses. Just look who this was! "Lafayette! Lafayette!" the Austrians shouted, as if they had just landed the biggest fish in the sea.

Of course this was a piece of bad luck, but optimist that he was, Lafayette could not realize how completely he'd lost his freedom. Carted off to prison, he was put behind bars and he stayed behind bars for five years, first in one country, then in another. The prisons were much the same—cold, damp, dark, filthy, rat-infested, dungeonlike. They were no better than the Bastille had been. Often kept in solitary confinement,

Lafayette was allowed no air or exercise, and he was watched. Twenty-four hours a day. During the day a guard stood on duty, peering in the little peephole in his door. At night a guard stood at the head of his bed, as if he were silently daring him to go to sleep. Of course to stay alive, he had to eat, no matter how revolting the food was. And he had to eat with his hands. Knives and forks were prohibited in case he'd try to commit suicide.

Suicide! Lafayette exclaimed. He'd never give them the satisfaction.

The guards snickered. But it must feel strange for a nobleman to eat with his hands.

Not at all, Lafayette replied coldly. He had often eaten with the Iroquois Indians in America and that was how they ate.

✥ Chapter Six ✥

For Lafayette the hardest part of prison was not knowing what was going on in the world outside. Where was Adrienne? And his children? And what was happening to the government? He didn't know about the terrible Reign of Terror, which began just three weeks after he'd been imprisoned. Those radical leaders were rounding up the aristocrats, lining them up at the guillotine. The king was beheaded on January 23, 1793; the queen shortly after. Sometimes fifty or sixty people a day had to submit to the guillotine. Adrienne was put in a Paris prison in what seemed to be a holding pattern. Every day she watched fellow prisoners being led to their death while she awaited her turn. Her mother and one sister were both executed, but Adrienne survived the terrorists. In 1794 a more moderate group took control of the government and, the next year, set Adrienne free.

She went straight home and gathered up all Lafayette's precious American possessions and buried them. Then she sent George, fourteen years old now, to America in care of George Washington. Adrienne might have gone to America too, but there was only one place she wanted to go. She was determined to join Lafayette in the Austrian prison of Olmutz where he was now being held. Virginie and Anastasie, who had been in the care of an aunt, insisted they go too. And with the help of American diplomats, they set out.

For Lafayette, one day was like another at Olmutz—the same inedible food, the same penetrating smell of the cesspool just outside his cell, the same sullen guards on watch. And then one October day in 1795 the cell door suddenly clanked open, and there stood Adrienne, Virginie, and Anastasie. Overjoyed as he was, Lafayette could scarcely comprehend what was happening. As the days went by, however, he could only marvel at how much more bearable prison life was when shared with his family. Although they were not allowed to be together all day, Lafayette still had time to catch up on what was happening to their friends and to France itself.

Perhaps now he began hearing more about Napoleon, France's new hero. The way Adrienne described him, however, he sounded dangerous. He has such a "halo of glory," Lafayette wrote a friend, he wouldn't be surprised to see him become the "master of France."

Indeed, he was on his way. But at the moment Lafayette was less interested in Napoleon than he was in Adrienne. She had become seriously sick but refused to leave Lafayette to seek outside medical help. Lafayette's American friends had been trying for five years to free him, but now with the news of Adrienne's health, they doubled their efforts. The emperor of Austria finally agreed to Lafayette's release on the condition that he never set foot in Germany again. The Directory (the present moderate government in France) agreed to his release as long as Lafayette stayed out of France.

So on September 19, 1797, the gates of Olmutz were opened and the Lafayettes were set free, but where would they go? They couldn't go to France, nor could they stay in Germany, and Adrienne was much too sick to make the long journey to America. So they settled in a community in Denmark where a number of French aristocrats, including Adrienne's sister, had established themselves after their flight from France. Lafayette was forty years old now, but his friends marveled. He hadn't changed at all. He still talked about liberty and was as enthusiastic as he had always been. Listening to him, his friends said, made them feel young again. But how, they asked, after five years in prison, could he still be so optimistic?

For two years the Lafayettes stayed in Denmark while Adrienne recovered her health, and Lafayette rested. He passed the days playing chess with a friend. George joined them and Virginie got married. Gradually Adrienne's health improved and since she was not considered as dangerous as her husband, she was allowed to go freely back and forth to Paris to take care of business matters.

Meanwhile, Napoleon had taken the army and sailed for Egypt, which he expected to conquer quickly. But nothing went right for Napoleon in Egypt. Of the fifty-six ships he had, eleven had been lost in confrontations with Britain. (Nine had surrendered.) As for men, he had lost approximately ten thousand, one-third of the original number. Still, when he reported back to France, he said, "All is well." At last he decided all would never be well in Egypt and he might do better to return to France and try his luck there. And since he was hearing rumors of trouble among the Directors, he thought he might even take over France.

In France, wildly enthusiastic crowds greeted him as the conquering hero, but in Paris he received a cold reception from the Directors. So he got rid of them one by one, and then set up a new government consisting of three men. He called this government the Consulate and, of course, Napoleon was the First Consul.

Adrienne was in France when all these changes were taking place and she decided this was the time for Lafayette to come home. She sent a message to him. "Now or never!" she said. So secretly, Lafayette, disguised as a messenger, re-entered France in 1799 and joined Adrienne at La Grange, the chateau and country estate that had belonged to Adrienne's family. But Lafayette's homecoming was not a secret that could be kept long. When Napoleon heard Lafayette was back, he threw a temper tantrum. The last thing he needed was the "hero of two worlds" competing with him for popularity. He told Lafayette to stay out of politics. Just stay out of his way, he said. He made sure Lafayette was not invited to any public functions.

Lafayette had not been back in France long when the news arrived that George Washington had died. Overcome with grief, Lafayette tortured himself with questions. Why hadn't he been at Mt. Vernon? Why hadn't he found a way to return at least once to America? How could the French remember Washington without referring to Lafayette? In America their names had always been coupled.

Of course, Napoleon even refused to invite Lafayette to the

memorial service the French gave for George Washington. But his son George sneaked into the ceremony and, hiding behind a pillar, listened so he could report back to his father. Lafayette's name was not mentioned once.

When Napoleon heard George had been at the service, he threw another temper tantrum. How could the Lafayettes still oppose him? After all, he was not only the master of France now, he was pushing into other countries, conquering pieces here and there, changing the map of Europe, and leaving devastation in his wake. He didn't worry about the dead. What were fifty thousand dead, he once asked, in comparison to *me?* It was for that *me* that Napoleon was racing over the countryside, collecting victories. Perhaps if he tried, he could even win over Lafayette. Accordingly, he let it be known Lafayette was free to call on him.

The two men met—Lafayette, the tall, imposing man, every inch a gentleman, and Napoleon, the short, rough-and-ready soldier with the unforgettable eyes. Prepared to be enemies, they were surprised to find they almost liked each other. Napoleon set out to be charming, but Lafayette determined that no matter how well they got along, he would not compromise, not even an inch. For Napoleon it was a new experience for someone to disagree with him openly, and he may have found it stimulating. In any case, from time to time he baited Lafayette.

"You must have found the ardor of the French for liberty very much cooled," Napoleon observed.

"They are in a state to receive it," Lafayette replied stubbornly. "They expect it from you, and it is for you to give it to them."

Napoleon tried other ways to bring Lafayette around. He offered him a seat in the Senate.

No, Lafayette replied. If he were a senator, he'd have to denounce the government and its chief.

What about being the French ambassador to the United States?

Lafayette shook his head. If he didn't wear his American uniform when he arrived in America, he said, he'd feel "as embarrassed as a savage in knee breeches."

Neither man gave in to the other. When in 1802 Napoleon asked the nation to vote on making him First Consul for life, Lafayette not only voted No, he told Napoleon how he was voting.

When on December 2, 1804, Napoleon was crowned emperor of France, Lafayette was not surprised. He'd seen it coming.

Napoleon was relentless in his pursuit of glory. Austria and Prussia submitted, and in 1805, Napoleon entered Berlin in triumph. At the time, however, Lafayette was absorbed with events closer to home. Adrienne's health, which she had never fully recovered since Olmutz, took a turn for the worse, and Lafayette couldn't bear to leave her side. Nor did Adrienne want him to leave. She was still so wildly in love with Lafayette that often she felt faint, she confessed, when she simply looked at him. Although Lafayette had always felt affection for Adrienne, at Olmutz he rediscovered her, falling in love as if for the first time. When she died on Christmas Eve, 1807, he had her room sealed off, leaving only a small hidden door so he could enter, meditate, and grieve.

Lafayette was fifty years old now. He walked with a limp, the result of breaking a leg when he slipped on ice. And he had gained weight. Still not as much as Napoleon had gained, he was proud to point out. He longed to visit America, but if he left the country, he knew Napoleon would never let him back in. Indeed, Napoleon was so in love with his own glory that he made the whole idea of glory seem sickening. Then in June 1812, he entered Russia with an army of five hundred thousand, but the Russian army plus the Russian winter defeated him. When he retreated, his army was only one-fifth of its original strength.

It was clear to Lafayette there was no way to rebuild France in the image of America as long as Napoleon was around. Other countries were asserting their independence and threatening Paris, so what were the French to do? Should they follow Napoleon into more wars? Should they desert him? Napoleon's younger brother, Lucien, speaking in the chamber, came to his defense. In a time of trouble, he said, everyone should stick together. If the people abandoned the emperor now, France itself would be dishonored.

This was too much for Lafayette. He rushed to the podium of the Chamber: "Do you dare to reproach us with failing in our obligations to Napoleon? Have you forgotten all we have done for him? Have you forgotten that the bones of our children and our brothers are strewn everywhere in witness of our loyalty? Three million Frenchmen have lost their lives in the service of the man who now wants to enter into the struggle against the whole of Europe. We have done enough for him! Enough!"

There was one more question: would Napoleon abdicate? It wasn't easy for Napoleon, but the next morning he did sign a paper announcing his abdication. He was taken to the island of Elba and Lafayette, who took a hard look at him as he left, said he looked like a "worn old despot."

Almost immediately the family of the former French king returned to Paris, and the brother of the executed king, an enormously fat man who had to be carried around in a chair, declared he was Louis XVIII. If Lafayette hoped his vision for France would be realized under this king, he was soon disappointed. It seemed like nothing more than the exchange of one tyrant for another. Indeed, it was like a game of musical chairs, for within a year Napoleon escaped and was back, claiming his old throne and his crown. Only now he was a changed man, he said. He was for liberty and equality and he wanted to support the constitution. Perhaps because he seemed preferable to their fat king, the French believed him and welcomed him. *"Vive l'emperor!"* they cried.

Napoleon kept up his act of being one of the people, but Lafayette was not fooled. Nor was he surprised when Napoleon did what he always did. He went back to war. His enemies, under the leadership of England's Duke of Wellington, had already assembled at the Belgian city of Waterloo. Napoleon was badly defeated but not the least humbled. He came back to Paris, showing his true colors. "I must be clothed with great powers," he said. "In fact, I must be made dictator."

Instead he was taken by the British to the more distant island of St. Helena where he moped away his last years. In France the ultra royalists, now that they had their king again, began striking down all those freedoms that Lafayette had tried so hard to preserve. The king did allow the Chamber of Deputies to continue, although it was a fractious body with Lafayette at the center of the contentions.

Indeed, the conflict between the royalist party and the liberty lovers became so intense that Lafayette often put himself in danger. When he was warned to be careful, he just scoffed. What difference did it make what happened to him? It was France that mattered. When a friend of his, a strong liberty man, made a rash speech in the Chamber and was ordered out of the room, Lafayette seethed. But when a unit of his old National Guard came in to forcibly remove the speaker, Lafayette stood up. Drawing himself to his full height, he stared at the guards as if he couldn't believe they would do such a thing. And suddenly they couldn't. Looking at Lafayette, they stopped in their tracks and the regular police had to be called in to do the job.

But in 1824 everything changed. In the elections of that year Lafayette was not chosen to represent any district. If he was no longer participating in the government, how could he pursue his mission for France?

He was sixty-six years old now, but he didn't feel one bit like retiring. A friend had recently returned from America and had brought back a sketch he'd made of the town of Fayetteville, North Carolina. It was the first town to be named for Lafayette so of course he was interested, even if he'd never see it for himself.

It was hard for him to stay on the sidelines. His self confidence had been shaken over recent years, and he found himself turning to friends more and more—old friends and new friends for confirmation of who he was. He was especially partial to independent young women who not only shared his political views, but were open in their admiration for him personally. Often they confided their problems to Lafayette, hoping he would mediate for them. And, of course, Lafayette not only welcomed such opportunities but encouraged the friendships and warmed to the many compliments that followed. He assumed a paternal tone in his letters, but sometimes his endearments and intimate expressions did not quite seem to conform with the father figure he was assuming.

In particular there was Fanny Wright, an outspoken young woman with uncompromising opinions on slavery, on women's rights, on religion and marriage. Indeed, she was so aggressive she antagonized many people, but Lafayette admired her independence and admitted her to a close place in his heart. As for Fanny, she attached herself so firmly to Lafayette that she thought nothing of spending weeks at La Grange, even when Lafayette's family became concerned she was becoming too dependent upon Lafayette. In any case, these two were able to give each other the kind of friendship each needed.

Much as Lafayette enjoyed his new friends, however, what he needed right now was a good strong dose of America. Then one day in 1824 a letter came from James Monroe, the president of the United States, and from the United States Congress. It was an invitation to travel to America as the "nation's guest." A ship would be sent to France to pick him up; all he had to do was name the port he wished to sail from.

Well, why not? Lafayette asked himself. Why ever not? Suddenly he felt younger than he had for years.

✤ Chapter Seven ✤

Being the "nation's guest" turned out to mean that for a year the country would turn itself upside down while everyone (if at all possible) came out to welcome him personally. Never had any visitor to the United States been received with such universal enthusiasm, with such genuine warmth. For those who had lived through the Revolution, here was their chance to recapture their youth. The younger ones, steeped in stories of the Revolution, could now touch history, all those memorable years they had missed. Children too young to know what was going on were told to remember the moment when Lafayette waved to them. Even the horse that was to pull Lafayette's carriage was asked to pay special attention. "Behave pretty now, Charley," the driver said. "You are going to carry the greatest man in the world."

It was Dr. Lewis, however, assigned to meet Lafayette as he entered New England, who said it best: "Sir, America loves you."

"And Sir," Lafayette replied, "I truly love America."

From the moment Lafayette set foot on American soil, the celebration of this love affair began. The guns at Fort Lafayette were the first to salute him, then the guns from the ships in the harbor. Church bells rang; the West Point band played "See the Conquering Hero Comes!" So many flowers were thrown in his path, it was as if all the growing things in America were rushing to meet him.

But it was the people, the thousands upon thousands of people, who moved Lafayette most: farmers who had traveled miles to see him, men holding children high on their shoulders, women waving handkerchiefs. All were smiling and shouting, all were young together again. Usually there were veterans who pushed themselves up to Lafayette, eager to share their war experiences. One veteran opened his shirt to show the scar on his chest. He got this at Brandywine, he said, the same day that Lafayette had been wounded. Lafayette was never one to give himself over to emotion, but with his old comrades in arms, the tears came as he embraced them, calling each one by name, for Lafayette had a fine memory.

During his year as a guest, Lafayette traveled the length and breadth of the United States, visiting every state. To enter every new city, he generally had to pass through a flowered arcade attended by a bevy of beautiful young women often dressed in white while long lines of children burst into song. Sometimes the ladies wanted to crown him with a wreath of laurel, but he found this so embarrassing he either ducked or took the wreath in his hand. There were receptions, hand shaking, speeches, and at night balls continued to early morning. Jefferson wrote Lafayette that he was afraid the country would "kill him with kindness," but Lafayette was far too happy to allow himself to feel tired.

Often to keep to their schedule, Lafayette, his secretary, and his son George, who were with him, traveled far into the night. Even at two or three in the morning they would come upon knots of people waiting patiently to greet him as he passed. Wherever he was, people hung on to him, hating to see him leave. If it was night, a delegation of citizens carrying torches would often accompany Lafayette and his party to the border of the next state.

Lafayette could not help but miss Washington. It didn't seem right that Washington wasn't beside him, sharing his joy in America. He must often have felt as he had in Albany so many years ago when he wrote to Washington, "Oh, General, why am I so far away from you?" Surely he never felt this loss more strongly than when he visited Mt. Vernon and went down into the tomb where George and Martha were buried. He went alone, stayed an hour, and was red-eyed when he came out. Coming to meet him was Custis, a relative of Washington. He presented Lafayette with a ring, containing a lock of hair cut from Washington's head after his death. The ring, he said, had always been meant specifically for Lafayette, who was so moved he could only manage the briefest thanks.

Perhaps the city which gave Lafayette the most elaborate ceremonies was Washington City. Right away Lafayette was impressed by the changes in Washington, such as the new buildings lining Pennsylvania Avenue. But he was especially proud of the republican tone of the capital. There were no sentinels, no guards on duty as there were in France. Cabinet ministers, he reported, often answered the door themselves. And in a meeting with the president, Lafayette noted there was no special chair for the president. Nor did the president dress differently from anyone else. He wore the same kind of blue swallow-tailed coat that all the men were wearing.

On December 9, Lafayette was escorted by a committee to the Senate Chamber. On the next day a committee of seventy-four conducted him to the House of Representatives, which was crowded with visitors, including the entire diplomatic corps—all but the representative from France who had been instructed to ignore Lafayette. The French representative gave as his excuse that he was mourning the recent death of Louis XVIII. Lafayette either could not or would not join the mourning. Besides, he was too busy listening to all the words of praise being showered on him by the American government. And not only words. In gratitude for all his services, Congress gave him $200,000 and a whole township of public land.

After his public addresses to both the Senate and the House, he was congratulated on his use of the English language.

Why wouldn't he speak English well? he asked. He was an American and had been in Europe only on a visit.

He was given one more present while in Washington. A little dog. Lafayette and the dog got along so well that Lafayette decided to take the dog on his travels.

If Washington City seemed changed (as indeed much of the countryside did), Yorktown, where the last battle of the Revolution had been fought, was not changed at all. To Lafayette, it looked just as he had last seen it. In spite of the years of peace, Yorktown appeared to be either getting ready for a war or recovering from one. The earth was torn up; the redoubts stood where they had been left. Moreover, there were plenty of soldiers about—old ones who had fought at Yorktown, young ones who had not fought anywhere. They were all there to celebrate the anniversary of this last battle. Washington's old tent was set up, looking just as it once had. Lafayette walked about, nodding. "Yes, I remember," he said. "I remember."

Lafayette was assigned to stay in Cornwallis' old quarters, which was visited by many anniversary participants. One group scouting around the premises came upon a large collection of unused candles saved, perhaps, for a victory celebration. That night the candles were placed in a circle and lighted in honor of their own anniversary. The men vowed they would not leave until every one of those British candles had burned out.

There was one man Lafayette had expected to see at Yorktown and still hoped to find somewhere in the South—his old bodyguard, Isham Blake.

Of course he visited Fayetteville, which had planned a great welcome for him, but he wasn't able to form much of an impression of the town. All he could see when he looked out from the carriage was water, running down the streets, sheets of water falling from the skies. And mud. The horses struggled through it, the carriage wheels sank in it. But the celebration went on as planned, for here was the man for whom the town was named. When would they have the chance to see him again?

Lafayette thought he'd met everyone in Fayetteville (if not in North Carolina), but early the next morning he was told he

had a caller. Perhaps before he even reached his caller, he heard that familiar half-whistle and there was Isham! The two men rushed into each other's arms, laughing, joking, pushing away all the years that had come between them.

✤ Chapter Eight ✤

The person he was most eager to see, however, was Thomas Jefferson. He had made arrangements to go to his home, Monticello, and the news spread quickly. On the morning Lafayette was due to arrive, lookouts on the road reported his approach. "He's coming," they cried. "He's coming." By the time his carriage was climbing the hill to the top where Jefferson's great house stood, the lawn around the house was crowded with people. It was a quiet crowd. None of the usual cheering. No huzzas. The people seemed to respect the historic moment they were witnessing: the meeting of two old heroes, the reunion of two old friends. Jefferson had become frail, and in a shuffling sort of way, he hurried down his front steps while Lafayette, limping, did his best to bound toward him. Both men were too overcome to do more than just call out the other's name.

Talk came later, and of course they had much to say. The intimacy of the occasion was only extended when Jefferson invited the Madisons and the Monroes to join them. Knowing this might be the last time they would be together, they discussed all that was closest to their hearts. When the Madisons returned home later, Dolly Madison remarked how young Lafayette still seemed. Of course he had gained weight, she said.

Lafayette's five-thousand-mile circuit of the United States was due to end in Boston on June 17 in time for Lafayette to lay the cornerstone for the new Bunker Hill monument. With all the parties and the welcoming along the way, it was a tight schedule, even if the traveling itself had not presented obstacles. In Georgia the roads stumbled into holes, teetered on bumps, and indeed were so rough that once Lafayette vomited. He looked forward, however, to a smooth ride when they headed north from New Orleans by steamboat up the Mississippi and then east up the Ohio to the Cumberland River. There were a few stops with the inevitable ceremonies on the way and a visit with Andrew Jackson in Tennessee, but for the most part Lafayette rested, looked at the scenery, and with his secretary, began to attack the mountains of mail that had accumulated.

A steamboat was a new experience for Lafayette. He'd seen his first one in New York Harbor and as always he was in admiration of what Americans could do. But no matter how wonderful a steamboat might be, it could have an accident. At midnight Lafayette's steamboat ran into a rock, hitting it with such a jolt that passengers were thrown out of their beds. George ran to the deck and when he found the boat was actually sinking, he rushed back to Lafayette who was calmly getting dressed.

No! George cried. There wasn't time for that. They were already taking people ashore in the ship's one lifeboat. Lafayette continued to dress while George fussed. The governor of Tennessee was in his bare feet and had lost his wig, George pointed out, and then he and the secretary took Lafayette by the arms and led him to the deck. Lowering him with his stiff leg into the lifeboat was an awkward business, but Lafayette managed. It was not until he'd been ashore for a while that Lafayette suddenly noticed George was not with them.

He began calling him. "George! George!" he shouted. When there was no response, he began pacing up and down the shore. "George! George!"

At last George, who had gone back to the ship to make sure all passengers had left, showed up. Lafayette relaxed. He pulled a mattress out of the water and prepared to use it as a bed.

What had he actually lost? His tall beaver hat. And all those unanswered letters—six hundred of them. He couldn't regret them. He would not have to answer them now, would he? But there was one thing more. His little dog. Where was he? Lafayette called, he whistled, and in the end he had to agree his little dog was gone. He had planned to take him home with him. Poor little thing—he'd never see France.

The next day, one of the largest steamboats on the river stopped and took the stranded passengers on board, delivering them two days later to Louisville.

Although Lafayette was on the final leg of his journey, it was a rather long leg with many appointments on the way. He made appearances in Illinois and Ohio, listening to speeches and making some of his own. Then came Wheeling (in what would later be West Virginia) and from there western Pennsylvania with two counties next door to each other, which he

wouldn't want to miss. Washington County and Fayette County. Lafayette could not help but take pleasure in the fact that like old friends, these two counties rubbed shoulders with each other.

Lafayette had scarcely entered Washington County when an old veteran came down the road to welcome him. And yes, Lafayette knew him. He got down from his carriage and gave the veteran his most exuberant greeting. For this was Robert Humphrey, the young soldier who had carried him off the field at Brandywine after he'd been wounded. Lafayette remembered, however, there had been two young men. Where was his partner, he asked?

John Lane, Robert told him, had since moved to Elizabeth. Lafayette would be going through Elizabeth on the way to Pittsburgh, and he'd likely see John sitting on the porch of the hotel where he spent much of his time.

Robert Humphrey stayed close to Lafayette during the rest of the day through the ceremonies at the county seat of Washington (or Little Washington, as they called it). The welcoming programs were much the same in every city Lafayette visited—the same music, the same pretty white-dressed girls, the same profusion of flowers, the same complimentary speeches, but Lafayette always acted as surprised, as attentive, as grateful as if he were hearing and seeing it all for the first time. Lafayette spent the night at the Old Globe Inn and then it was on to Fayette County, and to Bunker Hill.

It was now the end of May and there was nothing to do but drive day and night whenever possible. And no matter how much Americans disapproved, they would have to drive on Sunday. Sometimes Lafayette, his secretary, and George became so tired on these all-night drives that they fell asleep while the horses plodded on. But they arrived in Boston not only on time, but on the fifteenth of July, two days early.

Although the march to Bunker Hill was not to begin until 10 o'clock on the morning of July 17, Boston couldn't wait to start celebrating. At dawn on the seventeenth, all the church bells in Boston announced: This was The Day. Guns split the air with their rapid-fire salutes, for indeed how could there be enough noise to proclaim the fiftieth anniversary of what was the beginning of American history?

Seven thousand men marching in column led the way to the site of the celebration. Eight open carriages followed, each filled with veterans who had actually fought at Bunker Hill. Then came a barouche pulled by six white horses carrying General Lafayette. Officials came next, accompanied by bands, fifes, and drums beating in triumph. Then came the people. Two hundred thousand of them. Could the hill even hold them all? One tier of bleacher seats broke under the strain, but when the ushers said the seats couldn't be fixed, Daniel Webster, the speaker of the day who came as close to looking like God as a man could, took charge. "Anything can be done," he thundered. "Do it." And they did.

Lafayette had been given a silver trowel with which to dig a hole for the cornerstone of the monument. The ceremonies continued with a prayer, a hymn, and the address by Daniel Webster. Of course Lafayette had not taken part in the Battle of Bunker Hill, which along with the battle at Lexington, marked the beginning of the American Revolution. At that time Lafayette was still in France, seventeen years old, newly married, and dreaming of glory. But if he could have looked ahead to this day, he would surely have thought this was a supreme moment of glory. For there was the great Daniel Webster addressing *him* who, along with other veterans, was standing at attention.

"Fortunate, fortunate man," Webster cried to Lafayette. "Heaven saw fit to ordain that the electric spark of liberty should be conducted through you from the New World to the Old, and we who are now here . . . have all of us long ago received it in charge from our fathers to cherish your name and your virtues. . . . Those whose lives have been prolonged to the present hour, are now around you. . . . They raise their trembling voices to invoke the blessing of God on you and yours forever."

Lafayette had thought he'd be sailing for home soon after the Bunker Hill celebration, but he was told his ship wasn't ready. He'd be delayed. Of course there was plenty to do. He paid a good-bye call on John Adams; he visited Jefferson again; he made a flying trip to the two states he had missed on his travels—Maine and Vermont. In Maine he found another reason to praise Americans. In Wiscasset, Maine, he was served his first dish of ice cream. How wonderful America was! Then it was time to assemble all the gifts he had collected and make them ready for his trip home. There were so many souvenirs they had to be loaded on a separate ship: five wild geese he'd caught traveling up the Mississippi, wild turkeys, Devonshire cows, American partridges, petrified shells, bows and arrows and Indian dresses from Missouri, a map of South Carolina in a silver frame, a grizzly bear, a bull, two heifers, a boat, a sword from the New York militia, a bottle of water from the Erie Canal, a piece of the ship *Alliance* on which he

66

had twice crossed the ocean, a cane made from the first wooden marker at the grave of Dr. Joseph Warren, hero at Bunker Hill. And there was one more item. Lafayette had a trunk filled with American soil. When he died in France, he wanted American soil to cover his grave.

It was September before Lafayette could leave America. President John Quincy Adams invited him to stay at the White House and persuaded him not to leave until after his sixty-ninth birthday on September 6, 1826. On the night before his birthday, President Adams gave a farewell dinner for him, but the hardest part of the farewells came the next morning as he was actually leaving. He found the president and his cabinet assembled in the front hall to say good-bye.

"We shall look upon you always as belonging to us," the president said, "during the whole of our life, and as belonging to our children after us. . . . You are ours by that tie of love, stronger than death, which has linked your name for the endless ages of time with the name of Washington."

There was nothing the president could have said that would have meant more to Lafayette. He was so overcome he could not make the kind of graceful reply he was used to. Instead, though he was a tall man and John Quincy Adams was a short man, he flung his arms around the president. Then as he entered his carriage, he took a final look at the White House. The militia was drawn up in formation; flags were being lowered in salute. And on the porch of the White House, standing among the columns, was John Quincy Adams, a forlorn little figure, waving and waving.

✤ Chapter Nine ✤

Lafayette's family hoped he would settle down at the farm in peaceful retirement. He did settle, but not very peacefully; he was too busy watching the new king, Charles X. He and the king were the same age and had gone to riding school together as boys, but they shared none of the same ideas. Although Charles X had promised to uphold the constitution, he didn't actually uphold anything but the aristocrats. He restored their titles, later even requiring that the sons of noblemen dress in a distinctive uniform so their aristocracy could be quickly recognized. He restricted the right to vote to the wealthy and re-established the old law which gave the oldest son in a family the sole right to receive his family's inheritance.

Lafayette was outraged. Why should a baby who had done nothing except be born be presented with a title and his family's possessions? Nothing irritated Lafayette more than for people to use his title. When they called him "Marquis," he was quick to correct them.

"General," he would say.

Of course in America he was often called "Marquis," but

since Americans had no titles, it was almost as if they were calling him by his first name. Besides, they were showing pride in the fact that a French Marquis was fighting for them.

In Paris people were too angry to wish their king a long life. Certainly Lafayette didn't wish it. Besides, Lafayette resented his place on the sidelines. Then one day Charles X decided to review the National Guard. This was a mistake. The Guard went through its military maneuvers but it could not keep quiet. "Down with the Ministry!" some of the Guardsmen shouted, and if they didn't say, "Down with the King!" it was clear they thought it.

The next day the king abolished the National Guard altogether. This was too much for Lafayette. He had started the Guard. He loved it and every member in it. How could the National Guard be thrown away as if it were nothing? Not being in the government, Lafayette had little chance to be heard, but fortunately a seat suddenly became vacant in the Parliament, and he was elected to fill it. He was seventy years old now and was unsteady as he walked to the podium. But as soon as he began to speak, his friends smiled at each other. He'd lost none of his fire, had he?

Charles X could not make a move without aggravating the public further. When he appointed Prince Jules de Polignac as his prime minister, the aristocrats celebrated. Here was a man on their side, a man who had publicly refused to follow the Charter, a man who would surely restore their old powers. So when the liberty men complained that the people were not taking their rightful place in the government, what did the king do?

He dismissed Parliament just as he had dismissed the Na-

tional Guard. He hoped to win more support at a new election. Instead, the liberty men won this election by a large majority. Then what did the king do?

He did away altogether with Parliament, and he ordered all newspapers that supported liberty to be destroyed.

It was then that the people took over. Members of the old National Guard dragged out their uniforms, shouldered their muskets, and re-formed themselves. Parisians went into the streets, and while bullets flew around them, they dug up tiles of the pavement and built barricades. Everyone turned to Lafayette for directions as to what to do next. He was the one with experience, and he was the one who used the word first. "This is a revolution," he said.

It became known as the Revolution of 1830, and Lafayette was at the center of it. "My conduct at seventy-three," he announced, "will be what it was at thirty-two." Eventually this revolution ended the reign of Charles X. The question was, what next? Cries of *"Vive Lafayette!"* rang out over the city. He could easily have declared a republic with himself as president, but he hesitated. The last republic the French had tried had ended up in the guillotine and the Reign of Terror. Perhaps France still needed a monarchy, but this time it must be one truly based on the constitution.

People were talking about the Duke d'Orleans, cousin of the king, who had been in power the first time Lafayette returned from the American Revolution. This duke, it was said, was from another branch of the family and not at all like the others. For a while he had worked to support himself like any workingman in Paris. He had lived in America for two years and had known Washington. How could he be anything but a republican? Lafayette talked to the Duke. Of course he would uphold the constitution, he said. He promised to ban hereditary titles and property qualifications for voters. Whatever Lafayette proposed, the Duke approved. "I think as you do," he said.

Well, Lafayette thought, why not?

So the Duke was crowned, but he would not be called King; he would be known simply as Louis-Philippe. He certainly behaved as a true republican. He lived simply without fuss or display. In the morning he shaved himself and laid his own fire. In the evening he sat in his bedroom slippers, reading the paper. When a group of citizens came to his window and shouted for him (and they often did), he ran out on the balcony and led them in singing the national anthem, tapping his foot, waving his arms in time to the rousing tune. Louis-Philippe kept in close touch with Lafayette, writing to him every day. Best of all, he put Lafayette back in command of the National Guard. In his Guard uniform, riding at the head of his men, Lafayette was happy. At last France was on the right road.

As for Americans, they were electrified when they heard the news. Church bells were rung, guns fired, parades marched. It was *their* hero, *their* Lafayette who had taken the American Revolution all the way to France.

It was almost too good to last, and it didn't last. Being a republican king, Louis-Philippe decided, was not much fun. He was constantly asking himself: was he being republican enough? Besides, he was tired of running out to the balcony and bawling the national anthem whenever anyone called his name. Worst of all, people were making fun of him. Because his head was shaped like a pear, he was given the nickname "Pear" which also meant "stupid." Cartoons were appearing, showing Louis-Philippe as a puppet being held by Lafayette who was pulling the strings. Withdrawing from Lafayette, Louis-Philippe turned to the aristocrats, claiming he had made no promises to Lafayette. Indeed his change of heart was so sudden that people decided his republicanism had only been an act to get him on the throne.

For Lafayette, the last straw came when Parliament took away his command of the National Guard. When Lafayette went to the palace, the king received him with his usual friendship, offering to have the order withdrawn, changed, moderated in some way so he could retain his command.

Lafayette would have none of it. "Sire," he said, "your system of government is no longer mine. Many patriots in all countries are persuaded that where I am, liberty will not suffer hurt."

So he took his old seat in Parliament along with other liberty men, opposing the government, proposing changes. When he spoke, he limped but stood tall and erect as usual, courteous, charming, witty, but aflame with liberty, not only for France but for other countries where liberty was threatened—Poland, Portugal, Italy, Spain. La Grange became a haven for political refugees and a gathering place for friends of liberty.

Lafayette had at last decided a republic could probably not flourish in a monarchy, so of course he was discouraged. But not for long. "I was always of a hopeful nature," he wrote, "and hope is far from abandoning me." He would not give up. Liberty, he realized, could not be won once and for all. It had to be fought for over and over. And he continued to fight in spite of the fact that the ranks of the liberty men were thinning. Sadly, he attended funeral after funeral.

His best friend died in February 1834, and though it was cold and raw on the day of the funeral, Lafayette, seventy-six years old now, insisted on walking bareheaded behind the hearse all the long way to the cemetery. George begged him not to go, but Lafayette was stubborn. Limping along, he accompanied the hearse, then stood in the cold while numerous tributes were made in the cemetery. It was his custom to give an address or simply to shout out the name of his departed friend at the grave as if he were calling out the name of a good man who had gone.

When he reached home, he was not only chilled to the bone, he was so exhausted he went straight to bed, and George called the doctor. Lafayette was more sick than he realized and was not able to leave his bed for several months. Although he had his family around him (grown now to thirty around the dinner table), he also had a loyal little companion who never left his side. A small white dog, given to him by a friend to replace the one he had lost in America, was so devoted to Lafayette he would allow no one to touch his master's clothes except his valet. If Lafayette felt better, the dog danced around the bed. On his bad days, he acted as distressed as George.

In the spring Lafayette rallied enough to go out in his carriage for short rides. On one of these excursions he was caught in a thunderstorm and came home, soaked to the skin. He suffered a relapse and on May 20, holding in his hand a miniature of Adrienne and surrounded by his family and his little dog, he died.

For fifty years the streets of Paris had rung with cries of *"Vive Lafayette,"* so of course Louis-Philippe was worried about what would happen now that the people's hero was gone. The very sight of his funeral procession could cause an irruption of disorder, an angry demonstration against a government he had opposed. So Louis-Philippe ordered a full-scale military funeral for Lafayette. Blanketed on all sides with soldiers and their drawn bayonets, no one would be tempted to disrupt the proceedings. Behind the hearse Lafayette's valet marched, carrying a black velvet cushion on which his sword and epaulettes lay. Then came the family, followed by members of Parliament (but no Ministers of State) and finally there were three thousand members of the National Guard in full dress uniform, but without arms. At the church the coffin was carried inside by Poles whom Lafayette had befriended in their common fight for freedom. Now Guardsmen, who had served under Lafayette, came forward to touch the coffin as it passed, their last farewell to their old commander.

Then the procession moved to Picpus, a small out-of-the-way cemetery enclosed by tall stone walls behind a convent. This was the place Adrienne had discovered after the Reign of Terror where hundreds of those massacred, including her grandmother, mother, and sister, had been thrown into a common grave. She had made this small plot of ground into a private spot of consecration and here she was buried. Now Lafayette was laid beside her. In the final act of the ceremony, the American soil, which Lafayette had collected, was spread over the grave.

✤ Chapter Ten ✤

As soon as the news of Lafayette's death reached America, President Andrew Jackson ordered the same military honors be accorded Lafayette as had been accorded to Washington. Nothing would have pleased Lafayette more. When the twenty-four gun salute was fired at every army post in the nation and on every ship, it was almost as if Lafayette and Washington were joined in death as they had been in life. Flags were lowered to half mast; the halls of Congress were hung in black; army and navy officers wore arm bands of mourning for six months. Memorial services were held throughout America.

But for Americans the celebration for Lafayette was not limited to single occasions. Just as John Quincy Adams had once said, Lafayette *belonged* to America and should be remembered not only by living Americans, but by their children and their children's children. They built his name right into the land, a permanent testimony of their love for him. There are now ten Fayettevilles in the United States, eleven towns and fourteen counties named Fayette, countless numbers of streets, hotels, and schools that bear his name. Children born in the year when Lafayette was the "Nation's Guest" often acquired Lafayette as a middle name. He was, of course, a man who deserved to be honored for his fearless, unswerving support of his principles; a man who embodied the very idea of freedom. But he was also a man who had an enormous capacity for love and, in return, was loved.

Notes

p 1. A marquis is the title of a nobleman who ranks just below a duke, just ahead of an earl or count.

Joan of Arc was a famous French heroine who, dressed as a man, led the French against the English who were keeping Charles VII from the French throne. She restored Charles, but in the end the English accused her of heresy and burned her at the stake.

p. 10. Hessian. The British paid soldiers from Hesse, part of Germany, to fight for them.

p. 15. The dogs were Pomeranians.

p. 27. Benedict Arnold had a splendid record of bravery, but he was also a vain man. After a dramatic showing at the Battle of Saratoga, he expected Washington to do him more honor. When Washington was slow in recognizing him, Arnold sulked. When he was put in command of Philadelphia, he fell in with a group of Tories, particularly Peggy Shippen, whom he married. He persuaded himself that he would be a hero again if he betrayed the Americans. Perhaps he would be given credit for ending the war, he said. Whatever his so-called motivation, he took money from the British in return for handing over West Point. So, of course, he was branded a traitor.

When Andre was declared guilty of being a spy, he begged to be shot like a gentleman, not hanged like a common thief. Washington said NO. The American, Nathan Hale, who had been caught as a spy, was hanged by the British.

p. 39. Lafayette presented his Rights of Man and Citizens on July 11, 1789, just three days before the assault on the Bastille.

p. 40. Austria was one of those governments which wanted to keep ideas of the French Revolution from spreading through Europe.

p. 48. The French government, depending on who was at the head of it, was divided into two houses—the Chamber, which corresponds to our House of Representatives, and the upper house, variously called the senate or the House of Peers.

p. 52. Fanny and her sister followed Lafayette to America and joined him in some of his travels. But Fanny had her own agenda. She bought a large piece of land in Tennessee and settled slaves on it while she taught them about freedom.

p. 54. Many Americans took for granted that Lafayette's lame leg was the result of his wound at Brandywine. Actually it was the result of a leg he had broken in 1803 when he'd fallen on ice. A French doctor tried to heal it by putting it into a painful iron contraption which didn't work and left him lame for life.

Bibliography

Bedoyere, Michael de la. *Lafayette: A Revolutionary Gentleman* (New York: Scribners), 1934.

Brandon, Edgar Ewing. *Lafayette: Guest of a Nation A Contemporary Account of the Triumphal Tour of General Lafayette* 2 vols. (Oxford, Ohio: Oxford Historical Press), 1954.

Buckman, Peter. *Lafayette* (New York and London: Paddington Press), 1977.

Coombs, Edith J. (arranged by). *America Visited* (New York: Book League of America), N.D.

Fleming, Thomas. *Liberty! The American Revolution* (New York: Viking), 1997.

Gordon, Noel B. *Statue in Search of a Pedestal* (New York: Dodd Mead), 1976.

Gottschalk, Louis. *Lafayette Comes to America* (Chicago: University of Chicago Press), 1935.

Gottschalk, Louis. *Lafayette and the Close of the American Revolution* (Chicago: University of Chicago Press), 1942.

Gottschalk, Louis, ed. *Letters of Lafayette to Washington, 1777–1799* (Philadelphia: American Philosophical Society), 1976.

Headley, P.C. *The Life of the Marquis de Lafayette* (New York: A.L. Burt), 1903.

Horn, Pierre. *Marquis de Lafayette* (New York: Chelsea House), 1989.

Ketcham, D.C. *Marquis de Lafayette* (New York: A. L. Burt), 1903.

Kramer, Lloyd. *Lafayette in Two Worlds* (Chapel Hill, North Carolina: University of North Carolina Press), 1996.

Lafayette, Marie. *Lafayette Memoirs: Correspondence and Manuscripts* Published by his family. (Sanders & Otley), 1837.

Lafayette, Marie. *Lafayette in the Age of the American Revolution: Selected Letters and Papers, 1776–90* 5 vols. (Ithaca, New York: Cornell University Press), 1977.

Latzko, Andreas. *Lafayette: A Life* (Garden City, New York: Doubleday, Doran and Company, Inc.), 1936.

Levasseur, A. *Lafayette in America: Journal of a Voyage to the U.S.* 2 vols. (Philadelphia: Carey & Lea), 1829.

Loth, David. *The People's General* (New York: Scribners), 1951.

Oates, John. *The Story of Fayetteville* (Charlotte, North Carolina: The Dowd Press), 1950.

Roberts, Octavia. *With Lafayette in America* (Boston: Houghton Mifflin), 1919.

Rosenfeld, Richard. *American Aurora* (New York: St. Martin's Press), 1997.

Schom, Alan. *Napoleon Bonaparte* (New York: HarperCollins), 1997.

Whitlock, Brand. *Lafayette* 2 vols. (New York: D. Appleton & Co.), 1929.

✤ Index ✤